George Washington Visits

by Dennis Fertig
illustrated by Kellie Lewis

Glenview, Illinois • Boston, Massachusetts • Mesa, Arizona •
Shoreview, Minnesota • Upper Saddle River, New Jersey

ISBN-13: 978-0-328-38514-0
ISBN-10: 0-328-38514-X

2 3 4 5 6 7 8 9 10 VOEH 17 16 15 14 13 12 11 10

Daniel and Father were excited. Tomorrow, George Washington, America's greatest hero, would visit their town—Trenton, New Jersey. The town planned a big celebration.

2

BLACKSMITH

SEE
GENERAL
GEORGE
WASHINGTON
TOMORROW

Tonight, though, the springtime
skies over Trenton turned dark.
Big raindrops fell faster and faster.
"Daniel, let's hurry," Father called.

Father and son sprinted to a small barn near the town's center. It was Father's blacksmith shop. He used an iron key to quickly unlock the door.

When the door opened, Daniel could see huge piles of freshly picked flowers inside the shop. The flowers blew in the wind.

"Close the door fast," called Father.
"Don't let the flowers blow around."
Daniel shut the door. "I hope it doesn't storm tomorrow!" he said.

In a few moments, Daniel was handing flowers to Father. They were making a special sign. It was an iron frame filled with hundreds of flowers.

7

"Will General Washington see our sign?" asked Daniel.
"Yes, he will pass under it," said Father. "And remember,
he'll be *President* Washington in a week."

Daniel kept handing Father flowers.
Father asked for red blooms, yellow
blooms, and green leaves and stems.

9

Daniel liked helping. But he wasn't sure he liked
flowers. He wasn't sure if boys were supposed to.
Yet Father liked flowers, so it must be all right.

After hours of difficult work, father and son were finished. Father shoved the big sign up against the wall. The iron frame was heavy.

Daniel read aloud,
"December 26, 1776–January 2, 1777."
Daniel thought for a second.
"That was before I was alive."

Father said, "Yes, it was twelve years ago. I was a soldier then." Father frowned and looked serious. Daniel knew he was remembering the terrible war.

13

The war was the Revolutionary War.
Before it started, the British king ruled America.
Americans fought the war to be free. Americans won.

Daniel asked, "Father, did you know that America would win the war?"
Father smiled. "At first, I wasn't sure—until someone changed my mind."

"Who changed your mind, Father?"
Father answered, "George Washington."
"You knew him?" asked Daniel in amazement.

"Oh, I never spoke with him. But I was one of his soldiers. I did see him often then," Father said as he looked at the dates on the sign.

"On those days, we fought a battle here in Trenton," Father explained. "In the middle of a winter storm, we attacked a big British army."

"We won that battle. And I knew we would keep winning battles, because General Washington was smart, brave, and determined. I was right."

The next morning, it rained a little but then stopped. Father and other men moved the big sign. They set it up over the road into Trenton.

Later that day, Daniel and Father stood near the sign. Soon they could see George Washington on a white horse. Crowds cheered and cheered.

2

As George Washington rode under the sign, he looked toward Father. Then he looked again. Did he remember Father?

22

George Washington stopped his horse
and bent over to shake Father's hand.
"Thank you soldier for your brave service,"
George Washington said.

Were boys supposed to have tears in their eyes? Daniel wasn't sure. But Father did, so it must be all right.